NORTH DA

MW01535216

Take the Adventure & Explore

Fort Abraham Lincoln
state park

by Scott R. Kudelka

Adventure Publications, Inc.
Cambridge, Minnesota

DEDICATION

In memory of "Sergeant Major" Mark Kenneweg, whose passion for the history of Fort Abraham Lincoln State Park still resonates today.

To my partner and best friend, Angie, who inspired me to write this book!

To my parents, Roger and Shirley, who have always believed in me.

This book is for my niece, Jenny Kudelka Hanson, as she begins to explore and enjoy her own adventures in North Dakota.

Edited by Hope Klocker and Brett Ortler

Book and cover design by Jonathan Norberg

Photo Credits by photographer and page number:
Cover photo: Calvary Square and Missouri River by Scott R. Kudelka
Angie Becker Kudelka: 58, 80 **Scott R. Kudelka:** 8, 9, 14, 15, 16, 17, 18, 19, 22, 24, 33, 34, 35, 36, 38, 39, 42, 43, 44, 45, 47, 48, 49, 50, 51, 54, 57, 58, 59, 60, 61, 62, 63, 64, 65, 66, 69, 70, 71, 72, 73, 75 **Shirley Kudelka:** 4, 5 **North Dakota Parks and Recreation:** 10, 11, 21, 22, 23, 25, 26, 27, 28, 29, 30, 32, 37, 53, 56, 74 **State Historical Society of North Dakota:** 40, top photo, catalog #D0566; bottom photo, catalog #C1824, 43 (catalog #A5822), 45 (catalog #0410-043), 52 (catalog #0200-5x7-793), 53 (catalog #C1824-2)

10 9 8 7 6 5 4 3 2 1
Copyright 2008 by Scott R. Kudelka
Published by Adventure Publications, Inc.
820 Cleveland St. S
Cambridge, MN 55008
1-800-678-7006
www.adventurepublications.net
Printed in China
ISBN-13: 978-1-59193-181-2
ISBN-10: 1-59193-181-9

ACKNOWLEDGMENTS

Where do I start? Well, I want to thank and acknowledge everyone for the help they gave me in putting this book series together. First off, a big thank you to my family for their support, excitement and assistance with the creation of the North Dakota State Parks set of guidebooks.

I want to especially thank Doug Prchal and Donna Schouweiler with the North Dakota Parks and Recreation Department for their ongoing encouragement with this project and their support with the accuracy of the material. As I traveled across the state acquiring images, a number of people went out of their way to help me. This includes Henry Duray, Lorraine Schroeder and Dennis Clark at Icelandic State Park; Jim Loken at Beaver Lake State Park; Maureen Trnka and Dan Schelske at Fort Abraham Lincoln State Park; John Kwapinski at Fort Ransom State Park; Dick Messerly of Fort Stevenson State Park; Steve Crandall at Turtle River State Park; Larry Hagen and Bill Deming at Lake Metigoshe State Park; Eric Lang at Cross Ranch State Park; Dick Horner of Devils Lake; John Tunge of Lake Sakakawea and the staff of Lewis and Clark State Park. Thanks also to Erik Spencer, Mark Brown and Kris Dirk for help with maps and photos.

Thanks to Kelly Sorge for providing material and photos on Indian Hills State Recreation Area. From the North Dakota Game and Fish Department it was Dale Repnow, Brian Prince, Bruce Renhowe, Dan Halstead and Craig Bihrle; at the U.S. Forest Service it was Darla Lenz; and material on the U.S. Fish and Wildlife Service was reviewed by Ken Torkelson, Jackie Jacobson, Lynda Knutsen, Ted Gutzke, Joe Maxwell, Paul Halko and Dean Knauer. At the Lewis and Clark Interpretive Center it was Kevin Kirkey. From North Dakota Tourism, I want to thank James (Scooter) Pursley for help with their photo collection. Thanks also to Kit and Fay Henegar of Captain Kit's Marina.

Finally, I need to thank everyone at Adventure Publications for giving me this great opportunity. It is an experience that will stay with me forever. Thanks especially to my long-suffering and dedicated editors, Hope Klocker and Brett Ortler.

MY PASSION FOR PARKS

I grew up in southeastern North Dakota in a town of 500 or so people. Forman sits on the edge of the Red River Valley, close enough to see the rich agricultural land but stuck with a rockier terrain. My parents enjoyed throwing us kids in the back of a cramped camper on a 1960 green Ford pickup in search of a new adventure. Some of our best trips unfolded within North Dakota's borders. This was a great way to explore our home state and experience the unique characteristics of a prairie landscape.

Vivid memories of visiting state and national parks as a young boy still fill my head. The big trip of my youth was to the Badlands at around age eight, exploring a crumbling landscape where Theodore Roosevelt rediscovered his passion after the death of

Author at Little Missouri State Park

his wife and mother. In the various state parks, I pretended to be one of Custer's cavalry at the blockhouses of Fort McKeen, skateboarded along the rolling, curving roads in the riparian (floodplain) ecosystem of Turtle River and roasted marshmallows at Fort Stevenson Recreation Area before it became a state park. I also scrambled up the steep Pyramid Hill near Fort Ransom for a close-up view of the Viking statue; saw my breath on a cold morning at Icelandic and discovered aquatic life in creeks flowing into the Sheyenne River.

In the summer of 1986, I got thrown into the job of seasonal park ranger at Little Missouri Bay State Park, straddling the line between the Great Plains and Badlands. With no clue what this job was all about, I saw it as a once-in-a-lifetime experience. As the only employee of a 5,000-plus-acre park, this lifestyle charmed me and it didn't let go until the end of the century, when I finished my parks career as a full-time ranger. In between, I bounced around North Dakota working at Fort Stevenson, Cross Ranch, Lake Metigoshe and Icelandic. During that time I cross-country skied 104 days during the severe winter of 1996-97, helped build the Centennial Log Cabin at Cross Ranch and never took my service revolver out of its holster.

This book is a result of the work I did during my 15 years in the Parks and Recreation Department. A number of good people crossed my path in my life as a park ranger and played a major influence. Daryl Kleyer, a Sakakawea park ranger, took a chance on me more than once and gave me the job at Little Missouri Bay. Jesse Hanson, brother-in-law, mentor and the guy who introduced me to the Hensler Bar. Jesse and my sister, Lisa, always had a bed, meal and job when I was down on my luck. Doug Prchal was my late-night philosopher buddy and horse wrangler. Jim Loken, the one guy who believed I could soar higher than as a seasonal ranger at Fort Stevenson. Brad Pozarnsky, who allowed me to fly without boundaries. And Dennis Clark, Kevin Kirkey and Darla Lenz, three of my best friends, who were always willing to hear my stories and ramblings of life. To my brother, Brian, and my sister, Susan, who shared some of my best experiences exploring the state parks of North Dakota. Finally, to Chris, my other brother-in-law, who survived a chaotic 6-hour canoe trip on the Sheyenne River.

Author and father in the Badlands

TABLE OF CONTENTS

INTRODUCTION

History at Fort Abraham Lincoln is everywhere, crossing centuries and intermixing in vibrant shades. This is where the Mandan Indians thrived at their On-A-Slant Village for hundreds of years until a smallpox epidemic took a devastating toll on the people. Later, on their famous journey west, Lewis and Clark found the village abandoned and camped near the site. In 2007, Fort Abraham Lincoln State Park celebrated its centennial as North Dakota's oldest state park.

The U.S. military established Fort McKeen in 1872 as the railroad advanced across the frontier. After the construction of Fort Abraham Lincoln, Lt. Col. George Armstrong Custer and the 7th Cavalry arrived to take over patrolling from the infantry. On May 17, 1876, Custer and his men left the fort in a military campaign to control the Plains Indians but never returned.

Historical Tour of the Custer House

As the oldest state park in North Dakota, Fort Abraham Lincoln came into existence in 1907 and had its first major development during the 1930s under the Civilian Conservation Corps. Many of those original structures are still a significant feature of the park along with the numerous reconstructed buildings, including the cavalry post and earth lodges of the former Mandan village. These key historical sites are a part of an interactive interpretive and special event program. Visitors experience what life was like for a young American Indian in a female-dominated village and as a soldier on the western frontier far from home.

Fort Abraham Lincoln State Park is one of the most popular state parks for camping and is traditionally full on most summer weekends. Visitors enjoy a campground shaded by large cottonwood trees and a cooling breeze off the Heart River. There are two sleeping cabins for rent and a variety of picnic shelters to enjoy a family gathering. The Heart and Missouri rivers provide an opportunity for fishing, boating, and wildlife watching. Enjoy a hike on a challenging nature trail, a trolley ride from Bismarck, or take a bike ride on the asphalt path running through the park. Look for winter activities such as cross-country skiing, snowmobiling and the Custer Christmas.

Bismarck is the capital of North Dakota and its massive capitol building dominates the surrounding landscape. Located across from the capitol building is the State Heritage Center, where one can view the history of this prairie state through a large exhibition area. There are numerous historical sites within an hour's drive; visit Double Ditch Indian Village, the former Governors' Mansion, the Historic Mandan Depot and Five Nations Arts.

You can explore the Dakota Zoo, go for a Missouri River cruise on a paddleboat or enjoy the many opportunities Bismarck-Mandan offers for cultural activities, recreation, shopping and lodging. And while not everyone would think of gambling on the prairie, some may enjoy trying their luck at Prairie Knights Casino.

In winter, try downhill skiing and snowboarding at Huff Hills or snowmobiling on the 17-mile trail from the park to Fort Rice. To the north are Cross Ranch State Park and Nature Preserve, Lewis and Clark Interpretive Center and the Knife River Villages National Historic Site.

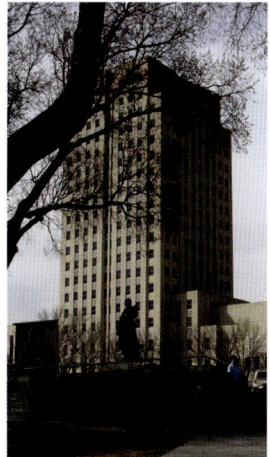

North Dakota Capitol Building

SCALE: 1" = 2000'

500' 0'   1000'   2000'

LEGEND:

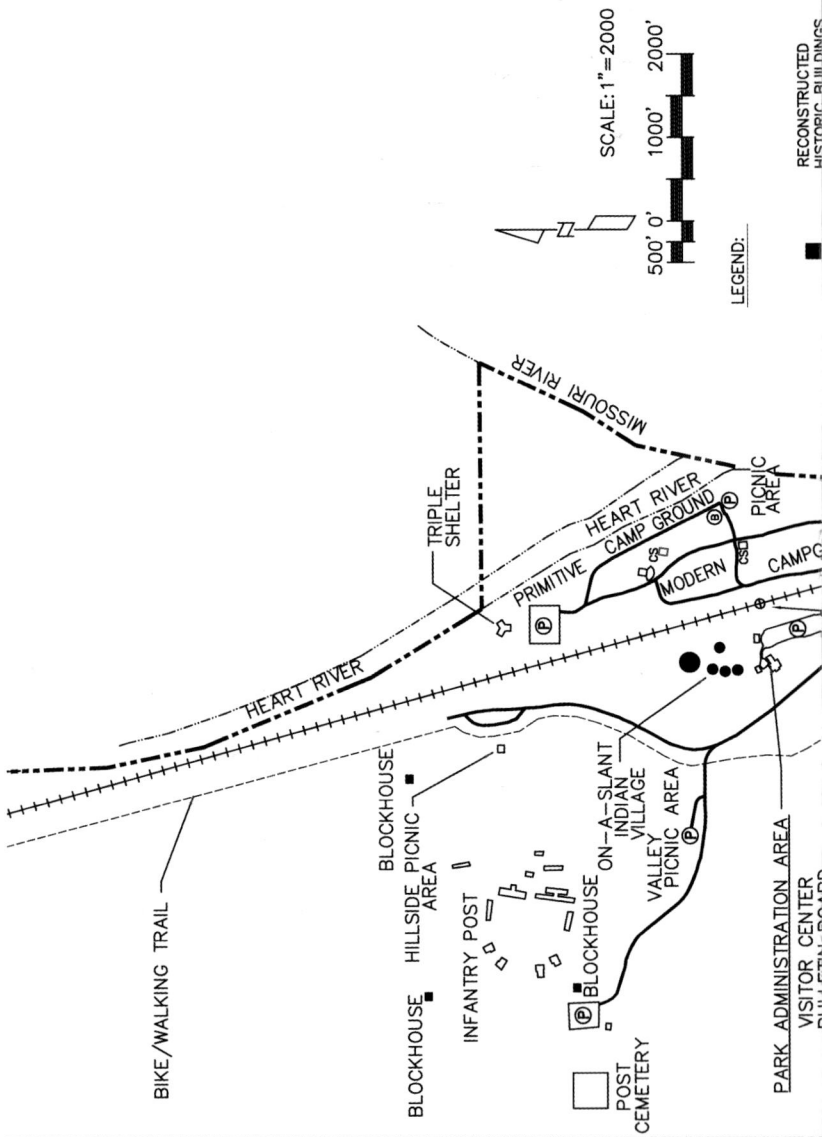

RECONSTRUCTED
HISTORIC BUILDINGS

MISSOURI RIVER

TRIPLE
SHELTER

HEART RIVER
CAMP GROUND

PRIMITIVE

MODERN

HEART RIVER

PICNIC
AREA

CAMPG

BIKE/WALKING TRAIL

BLOCKHOUSE

HILLSIDE PICNIC
AREA

INFANTRY POST

BLOCKHOUSE

BLOCKHOUSE

ON-A-SLANT
INDIAN
VILLAGE

VALLEY
PICNIC AREA

POST
CEMETERY

PARK ADMINISTRATION AREA

VISITOR CENTER

Legend:

- ℗ PARKING AREA
- cs COMFORT STATION
- Ⓑ BULLETIN BOARD
- ⌂ AMPHITHEATER
- ·········· TRAILS
- ╫╫╫╫╫ RAILROAD TRACKS
- ━·━·━ PARK BOUNDARY
- ━ ━ ━ RIVER BOUNDARY

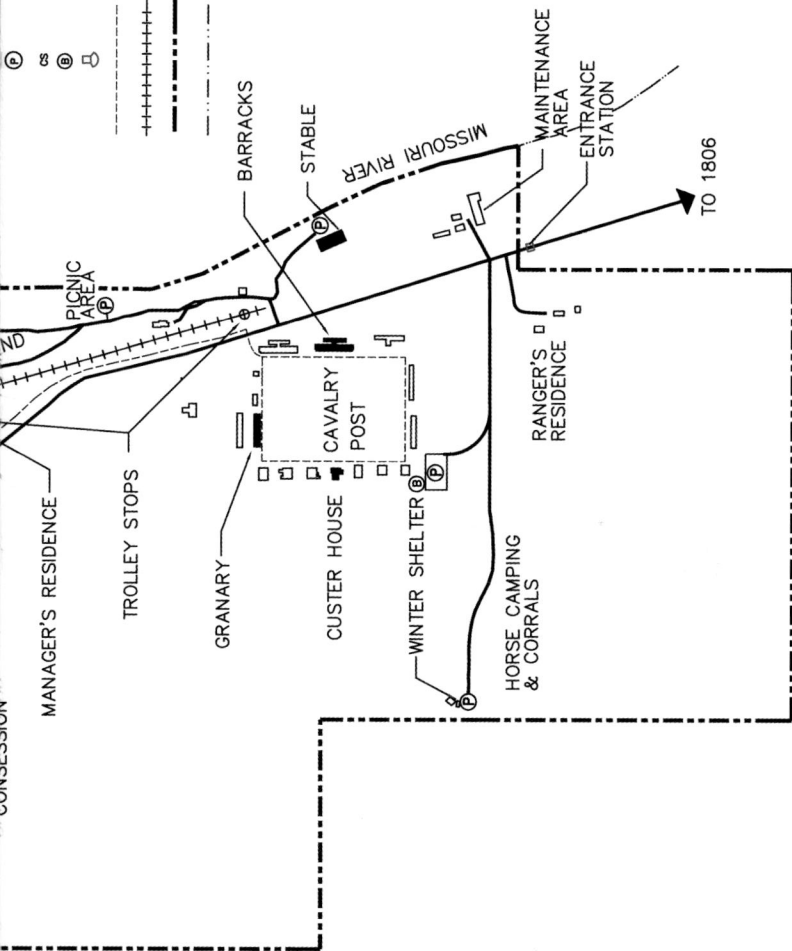

BARRACKS

STABLE

MISSOURI RIVER

MAINTENANCE AREA

ENTRANCE STATION

TO 1806

PICNIC AREA

MANAGER'S RESIDENCE

TROLLEY STOPS

GRANARY

CAVALRY POST

CUSTER HOUSE

WINTER SHELTER

RANGER'S RESIDENCE

HORSE CAMPING & CORRALS

CONCESSION

PARK AT A GLANCE

Location/Directions 7 miles south of Mandan on ND 1806. This park rises off the floodplain of both the Heart and Missouri rivers and reaches into the rolling hills.

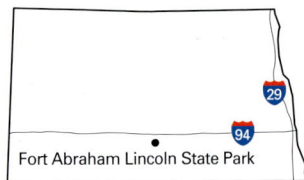
Fort Abraham Lincoln State Park

From Mandan take ND Hwy. 1806 south for 7 miles. The road will take you around to the south entrance. Turn left into the park.

From Fort Yates take ND Hwy. 24 north for 54 miles. The road turns into ND Hwy. 1806. Turn right into the park.

Contact Information

4480 Fort Lincoln Road, Mandan, ND 58554
701-667-6340; falsp@nd.gov

Established March 2, 1907

Size 1,006 acres of Heart River floodplain which spreads along the Missouri River and includes wooded areas and former mixed-grass prairie sections

Visitor Services

- museum and visitor center
- restored historic buildings: Custer House, commissary, barracks, granary, horse stables and infantry post blockhouses
- On-A-Slant Mandan Indian Village and earth lodges
- interpretive, guided tours and historical programs
- meeting room rental
- special events and an old-time melodrama
- trolley service
- campgrounds
- sleeping cabins

- picnic shelters, playgrounds
- self-guided nature, hiking and multi-use trails
- horseback riding and trail riding facilities
- shore fishing and accessible path
- gift and book shop
- winter activities and state snowmobile trail head

Camping
- 95 RV and tent sites open year-round

Things You'll Want To Do

- Visit the Custer House and other reconstructed buildings at Fort Abraham Lincoln where Lt. Col. George Custer and the 7th Calvary were stationed immediately prior to the Battle of the Little Bighorn.

- Step back in time and visit On-A-Slant Indian Village, originally inhabited by Mandan American Indians, or see re-created American Indian earth lodges. Or come to the Visitor Center and Museum to learn about the history of the region, including exhibits about the Mandan American Indians, the Lewis and Clark expedition and Custer and the 7th Calvary.

- Enjoy camping near the Heart River, have a picnic at one of the shelters, or hike the Ridgeline Nature Trail to explore the park's flora, fauna, and geology.

- Participate in one of the park's interpretive programs, meet the park's full-time historian, and participate in special events such as the Custer Christmas, or old-time Melodrama.

GETTING TO KNOW THE PARK

VISITOR CENTER/MUSEUM

Explore the history of the Mandan, Lewis and Clark, Custer and the 7th Cavalry and others who have made an impact on the history of Fort Abraham Lincoln State Park.

Open April through end of October
Times 9 am–5 pm with extended hours in summer
Features interactive exhibits on various time periods, historical presentations, videos

Visitor center/museum

ON-A-SLANT INDIAN VILLAGE

For over 200 years this was a prospering village of Mandan Indians who grew crops along the Heart River floodplain and hunted the great bison herds of the Great Plains. The sloping terrain gave the village its name and there were up to 85 earth lodges here with a village population of 1,000 people. As the southernmost village of nine other Mandan villages, the Mandan believed On-A-Slant was the center of the universe. When a

Original Civilian Conservation Corps Bridge to the On-A-Slant Village

smallpox epidemic devastated this village, the Mandan abandoned it and moved upstream to eventually join the Hidatsa on the Knife River. It was in an advanced state of decay by the time Lewis and Clark sighted the village in 1804.

FORT ABRAHAM LINCOLN

Lt. Col. George Armstrong Custer and the 7th Cavalry left from Fort Abraham Lincoln on a spring day in 1876 to force a number of Plains Indian tribes back onto the reservations. Custer and many of his men never returned, marking the beginning of the end for Fort Abraham Lincoln. Established early in 1873 to protect both the railroad workers and settlers, the fort was eventually abandoned near the turn of the century. Local settlers tore down all of the original structures for personal use, but today visitors can tour a number of reconstructed buildings.

FORT MCKEEN

Sitting on a hill overlooking the confluence of the Missouri and Heart rivers, this was the first military base located at the present-day park. Fort McKeen was established in 1872 as an infantry post to protect the survey crews of the Northern Pacific Railroad and the first settlers trickling into the Dakota Territory. But Fort McKeen was destined for a short life. After only six months, Fort McKeen lost its own identity and became part of Fort Abraham Lincoln, a cavalry post. Today the fort is identifiable by three wooden blockhouses looking over the surrounding terrain.

SLEEPING CABINS

Two semi-modern cabins at Fort Abraham Lincoln allow visitors to enjoy the rustic fun of camping while still enjoying some of the comforts of home. Both cabins are in a great location to enjoy all the recreational opportunities found in the park.

Sleeping cabin

- 2 cabins, adjacent to primitive campground and Heart River
- each cabin sleeps up to 5 people, and includes a loft for rustic charm
- has lights, heat and a deck, with comfort station and water hydrant nearby
- picnic table and fire ring outside
- one cabin is accessible to those with disabilities
- surrounded by a thick forest; good fishing close by in the Heart River

Available May 21–Sept 30

Fee per night (prices subject to change)

Reservations make reservations by calling 1-800-807-4723 or visit www.parkrec.nd.gov

COMMISSARY STOREHOUSE

If you're looking to hold a special gathering for a large group of people in a historic setting, this is the place for you. The reconstructed commissary offers a variety of features for both formal and informal parties.

- located on northwest edge of cavalry post
- this group meeting facility accommodates up to 200 people
- equipped with modern bathrooms, sink and refrigerator
- commissary available year-round
- rental fee: per day (prices subject to change)
- bookstore and souvenir shop inside; contains one of the finest collections of books on George Custer's 7th Cavalry and the American Indians of the Great Plains
- history exhibit of the fort's commissary

Commissary

Round CCC Picnic Shelter

PICNIC SHELTER

There are a variety of shelters available throughout the park for both a rental or on a first-come, first-served basis. Visitors can rent either the triple shelter or winter shelter.

- triple shelter is located on north end of campground areas, has scenic view of Heart River
- winter shelter located west of Cavalry Post on a dead-end gravel road
- rental fee: per day charge, prices subject to change
- 4 Civilian Conservation Corps shelters available on a first-come, first-served basis; 2 located at end of main road and 2 in campground

Triple shelter

FORT LINCOLN TROLLEY

Travel to the park area in style! Experience a form of transportation not often seen in modern times. The ride will take you across a bridge and trestle crossing from 1898 as the track runs along the scenic Heart and Missouri rivers.

Schedule Memorial Day–Labor Day
Starts Third Station Depot in Mandan
Ends State Park Station
Distance 9 miles
Cost $5 for round-trip ride, prices subject to change
Departs daily on the hour 1–5 pm from Mandan Station; departs on the half hour, 1:30–5:30 pm, from State Park Station

Fort Lincoln Trolley

ACTIVITIES

Visitors can enjoy a diverse selection of recreational opportunities on a variety of trail systems found throughout the park. Go for a 1–1 1/2 hour hike on the nature trail winding through the prairie blufflands and woody ravines. Numerous interpretive sites tell the environmental story of Fort Abraham Lincoln. Try biking, inline-skating, walking or jogging on a paved recreational trail running from the park to Bismarck/Mandan. In addition, horseback riding is a popular activity and is allowed west of the main park road. Enjoy the interpretive trails and history of the Cavalry Post, the Infantry Fort and the Indian Village site.

HIKING/BIKING

Ridgeline Nature Trail

To get a close-up view of the park's flora and fauna, and its geological and historical features, go for a hike on this self-guided interpretive trail crisscrossing a number of ecosystems. Early in the morning is the best time of day for observing wildlife and bird species.

Trail length 3/4 mile (1.2 Kilometers)
Estimated Walking Time 1–1 1/2 hours
Start Civilian Conservation Corps Picnic Area below Infantry Post, follows a loop back to picnic area
Elevation 1,750–1,900 feet above sea level
Features interpretive sites on historical, natural and geological aspects of the park
Check Out guidebook describing each interpretive site, available at the trail head or the Civilian Conservation Corps (CCC) Museum

Interpretive Sites

Wild Rose pink flowers of this western Woods' rose have a delightful fragrance and develop red fruits (hips) by late summer
Poison Ivy beware of oil on this plant; compound leaves divided into 3 leaflets; small, white, waxy berries eaten by birds and wildlife
Drought-Resistant Species look for plants such as prickly pear cactus and yucca, which grow well in dry areas

Juneberry purplish-blue berry of this shrub is enjoyed fresh or in pies, jelly and jam

Wooded Ravine on north-facing slopes, including green ash and bur oak due to moisture runoff from prairie and protection from strong winds

Lichen-covered rocks combination of algae and fungus forms the gray-green and orange scale-like growths on rocks; algae provides food, fungus gives support and stores water

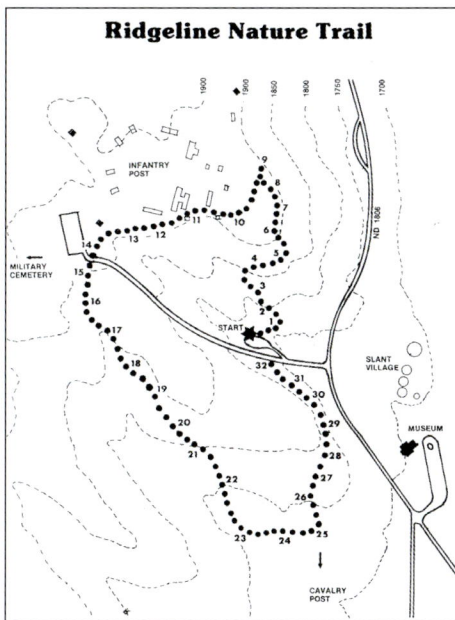

Ridgeline Nature Trail

Little Heart Butte this landmark of high, distinctively shaped hills guided American Indians and early explorers

Rocky Mountain Juniper berries and leaves boiled by Dakota and other Plains Indians as cough remedy; a juniper post representing the "first man" stood in center of Mandan villages

The Post Trail former wagon road linked cavalry and infantry posts and is the start of the Custer Trail; General Armstrong Custer led the 7th Cavalry on this trail to the Little Bighorn River in 1876

Mixed Grass Prairie short and mid-size prairie plants grow here, including blue grama grass and thread-leaved sedge

Leadplant part of pea and legume family, adds nitrogen to soil through bacteria in root nodules

Glacial Boulders glaciers carried these granite rocks here more than 10,000 years ago from Canada

Sage plant made into tea for stomach ailments or burned like incense at religious ceremonies by American Indians **Floodplain and Terraces** due to centuries of flooding, terraces formed–including

Ridgeline Nature Trail naturalist hike

the one holding the campground and a second at the cavalry post site

Millennium Legacy Trail

In 1999, The Millennium Legacy Trail Program designated one legacy trail for each of the 50 U.S. states, along with the District of Columbia and Puerto Rico. Each trail is accessible to people of all abilities represents the spirit of the state and reflects the heritage and culture of the community.

This is North Dakota's legacy trail and this hard-surface trail runs from Fort Abraham Lincoln State Park into Mandan. From there you will be able to connect with other trail sections throughout Bismarck and Mandan. Visitors of all ages will enjoy this combined 35-mile plus trail system on both sides of the Missouri River.

Hiking the Millennium Legacy Trail

Trail Length 12 miles to Ward Indian Village in Bismarck
Start Park Trolley Station
Activities walking, jogging, biking, in-line skating, (no motorized vehicles)
Check Out scenic views of Heart and Missouri rivers

Lewis and Clark Legacy Trail

- 5-mile single-track, non-motorized, trail located primarily in uplands north of Fort McKeen blockhouses

- trail head adjacent to paved multi-purpose trail, Fort McKeen site parking lot and Civilian Conservation Corps Visitor Center

- trail features 3 segmented loops to provide different length options

- features along trail include scenic views of the Missouri and Heart River valleys, woody draws, rolling prairie and a variety of plant species, wildlife and birds

Fort Abraham Lincoln State Park LegacyTrail

Proposed Trails
Phase 1
Phase 2
Mowed

All trail distances are approximate miles

Approximately 5.2 total miles of trail

Trail map

- unique opportunity to retrace steps of the Lewis and Clark expedition of 1804-'06

- North Dakota U.S. Senator Kent Conrad initiated the Lewis and Clark Legacy Trail Program to commemorate the Lewis and Clark Bicentennial

CAMPING

- full service camping from the weekend before Memorial Day through the end of September

- limited service available year-round

- during summer, contact campground hosts at site 10 in Modern Loop

Modern campground area

- primitive campground loop located on northeast edge

Modern and Primitive Campground

- located on the floodplain of the Heart and Missouri rivers; take right at Trolley stop, off main road

- modern loop located first, consisting of sites 1–57

- primitive loop off to right near Heart River shoreline, consists of sites 58–94

- campground well-shaped by a canopy of cottonwoods, green ash and other trees

- 2 comfort stations located in modern campground, hot showers and flush toilets available

- amphitheater for interpretive programs located between modern and primitive loops

- sewage dump station located on west road of modern loop

- other features: volleyball court, playground and shore fishing

Reservations

- 20 sites in modern loop

- 10 sites in primitive loop

- reservations fill up fast on most summer weekends

- call 1-800-807-4723 or visit www.parkrec.nd.gov

- reservation line opens first Tuesday of April

- reservation fee (price subject to change)
- all reservations must be made by credit card
- please do not camp in a site marked "Reserved" unless you have a reservation or consulted a park ranger

CUSTER TRAIL RIDES

A guided horseback ride harks back to a time when the 7th Cavalry was posted here and rode these hills.

Horseback riding

Schedule sunrise to sunset, 7 days a week during summer
Cost $12.00 per hour, prices subject to change
Location register at commissary/gift shop
Phone 701-667-6385

- children must be at least 7 years old
- for groups of 10 or more please call ahead

GEOCACHING

- the latest outdoor craze combines a treasure hunt with the use of high-tech GPS (global positioning system)
- participants look for hidden caches using latitude/longitude coordinates from various websites
- cache is tucked into a natural hiding spot (hollow log or boulder)
- may take 1 item and leave similar reward behind
- www.geocaching.com

FISHING

An accessible shoreline path is found in the campground. Try your luck at catching walleyes or northern pike.

WINTER ACTIVITIES

As the "banana belt" of North Dakota, the Bismarck-Mandan area experiences fairly mellow weather during the winter, yet still receives enough snow to make this season interesting. Fort Abraham Lincoln State Park offers a number of activities during the winter. Snowmobilers and ATV riders will enjoy the 17-mile Roughrider Snowmobile Trail. The trail heads south to the Fort Rice State Historic Site. There are also opportunities to get off a "manmade trail" by strapping on a pair of cross-country skis or snowshoes. If you are looking to do some downhill skiing, go south to Huff Hills Ski Area.

Cross-country Skiing and Snowshoeing

Even though the park staff doesn't maintain a groomed ski trail there is plenty of terrain for both cross-country skiing and snowshoeing. Both are becoming more popular winter activities and allow visitors to explore the park on their own.

Cross-country skiing in park

The best location for wind protection and snow depth is the campground and picnic area on the Heart River floodplain. Visitors can leave their vehicle in the museum parking lot and take the steps downward. If you are looking for a little more exertion, head out from the Cavalry Square into the rolling hills surrounding Fort McKeen.

Snowmobiling

A well-groomed trail runs south for 17 miles along an old railroad bed from Fort Abraham Lincoln to the Fort Rice State Historic Site. This National Recreation Trail was dedicated in 1979. Both

Snowmobiling on state trails

ATV and snowmobilers can use the trail. Please respect other visitors and users of Fort Abraham Lincoln.

Park users can warm up and rest at the winter shelter west of the Cavalry Square. Visitors will enjoy the crackling fire.

Please stay on all marked state trails and respect private property.

Downhill Skiing

Huff Hills Ski Area is located 16 miles south of Mandan and offers 4 lifts and sixteen ski runs. There are ski runs for everyone, including green (easy), blue (medium) and black (expert) trails. There is a 450-foot vertical drop and the longest run is 3,300 feet. On the bunny hill there is a tow rope.

A three-floor rustic chalet features a lunch café, fireplace and modern restrooms. Visitors can experience scenic views of the Huff Hills and use the sack lunch area and storage lockers.

Ski and snowboard rental, lessons and equipment repair services are available.

Contact
701-663-6421; www.huffhills.com

EVENTS/PROGRAMS

Fort Abraham Lincoln offers a wide range of special events, including the American Legacy Exposition and the Custer Christmas. History comes alive in the form of cavalry charges, American Indian dances and sleigh rides on a crisp December day. Most of the special events revolve around the Cavalry Square or the On-A-Slant Village site. Throughout summer, visitors can explore stories of the Mandan and be part of an old-fashioned melodrama.

AMERICAN LEGACY EXPOSITION

Learn about the park's two distinct cultures at Frontier Army Days and the Nu'Eta Corn and Buffalo Festival. Witness the sights and sounds of an 1870s military encampment and learn how the Mandan prospered along the Heart and Missouri rivers for more than two centuries.

Date last weekend in July
Time 10 am–7 pm
Location Cavalry Square and On-A-Slant Village site
Events old fort life presented through cavalry, infantry and artillery soldiers, along with laundresses and scouts

American Indian dance

- encampment set up on parade grounds with authentic tents and gear

- cannon drills, cavalry charges and mustering by infantry soldiers

- children's games, races and interpretive tours

- the spirit of the Mandan highlighted through demonstrations and presentations of this unique culture

- variety of foods relating to the two cultures, including bison

CUSTER CHRISTMAS

The Christmas holiday was an important time for the soldiers and families living at a frontier fort of the 1870s. On the second weekend in December the Custer House and enlisted men's barracks come to life with decorations and the celebration of Christmas. Visitors will welcome an 1875-style Christmas as enjoyed by General George Armstrong Custer.

Date second weekend of December
Time noon–4 pm
Location Cavalry Square
Activities Victorian Christmas decorations on display throughout the Custer House, barracks and commissary

- tours of buildings by historical interpreters in period costumes
- enjoy the smell of gingerbread, taste of hot apple cider, sound of carolers and sight of decorated Christmas trees inside
- sleigh rides and more family fun

Cannon drills

Cavalry drills

MELODRAMA

This type of drama harks back to an era when the most important form of entertainment involved everyone, including the audience. Enjoy an entertaining evening of "Villains and Heroes" performed by the Fort Abraham Lincoln Dramatic Association. Actors include the fort's soldiers and laundresses, along with volunteers.

Date mid-June to beginning of August, Thurs–Sat evenings
Time 7:30 pm
Location granary at Cavalry Square
Activities historical performance takes visitors back to late 1800s

- pre-show entertainment includes local music talent and Dramatic Association members
- enjoy root beer and popcorn

SPECIAL EVENTS

The staff of Fort Abraham Lincoln and the Foundation put on large and small events, all of which celebrate what makes this park special.

Stories of the Mandan

Experience contemporary presentations, demonstrations and American Indian storytelling with songs and sign language at the Council Lodge at On-A-Slant Village.

Date June–August

Storytelling at On-A-Slant Indian Village

Fort Lincoln Road Race

Runners will race on a path along the bluffs overlooking the scenic Missouri and Heart rivers. They will see the On-A-Slant Village, once home of the Mandan Nation, known for its strong runners.

Date third weekend in June

Fort Lincoln History Symposium

Both professional and amateur historians, scholars, authors and archeologists gather to learn more about the history of the Mandan Nation and General Custer's 7th Cavalry.

Date second weekend in July

The Haunted Fort

It was a dark and scary night. Go for an eerie, guided tour of three buildings on Cavalry Square. Not for the faint of heart. People say Libby Custer awaits the return of General Armstrong Custer from the Valley of the Big Horn River. This is only part of the tradition of haunted Fort Abraham Lincoln.

Date third weekend in October

INTERPRETIVE PROGRAMS

Interpretive programs have played an important role at Fort Abraham Lincoln State Park for many years, dating back to the outdoor drama "Trail West" in the 1950s. The pageant told the story of Custer's adventures from commanding Fort Abraham Lincoln to his death at the Battle of the Little Bighorn. Today visitors can explore the history of the park's cultural sites through guided tours led by costumed interpreters with full dramatic flair. Visitors also have the opportunity to enjoy amphitheater programs and a variety of children's games.

Living History Tours

In 1874 this two-story Victorian house on the western frontier became Lt. Col. George A. and Libby Custer's first real home. Today the restored wood-frame house is decorated with period furnishings and artifacts. In addition, a number of buildings have been rebuilt on Cavalry Square. Visitors will find uniformed soldiers and laundresses guiding historical tours through the Custer House and central barracks.

Hours Memorial Day weekend–Labor Day: 9 am–7 pm daily; after Labor Day to end of October: 9 am–5 pm daily
Features living history tours of various reconstructed buildings
Buildings include Custer House, commissary storehouse, enlisted men's barracks, granary and stable
Gift shop in commissary

On-A-Slant Living History Tours

Home to the Mandan for two centuries, this American Indian tribe lived in earth lodges, planted gardens on the floodplain and hunted bison. Today a number of the earth lodges and the ceremonial lodge have been rebuilt.

Dates Memorial Day weekend through Labor Day
Times 9 am–7 pm
Features guided tours by park historians every half-hour, exhibits on the Mandan way of life, gardens and religious activities.

On-A-Slant village tour

Ceremonial lodge

NATURE

Forested river floodplains, mixed-grass prairie and woody draws are the three major ecosystems at Fort Abraham Lincoln State Park. Pushing into one river bottom forest is the confluence of the Missouri and Heart rivers, a rare sight in North Dakota. This ecosystem is dominated by large cottonwood trees and a variety of understory shrubs. Moving upward into the park is a rolling mixed-grass prairie, sloping down into heavily vegetated woody draws. The three ecosystems flourish with a diverse selection of plant species.

RIVER BOTTOM FOREST

One of the most valuable parts of a river ecosystem is its floodplain, allowing high flows of water to spread out across the landscape. On the Missouri and Heart rivers, this resulted in a forested environment characterized by large cottonwood trees.

Continued deposits of new soil create the perfect environment for growing cottonwoods and willows. As time goes by, organic matter builds up, allowing for a richer level of nutrients in the soil. Soon other tree species begin to take hold, including green ash, boxelder, American elm and bur oak.

Bottomland forests and upland native prairie are both part of the landscape

At one time the Missouri River sat higher on the landscape, and today you can see a number of former floodplains rising above the current one. Called terraces, they spread up and down the part of the Missouri river still in its natural state. One such terrace holds the cavalry post.

MIXED-GRASS PRAIRIE

Both short-and tallgrass plants thrive together in this transition zone between the two distinctive native prairie ecosystems. This environment is the result of a number of specific circumstances, including the amount of moisture and soil types.

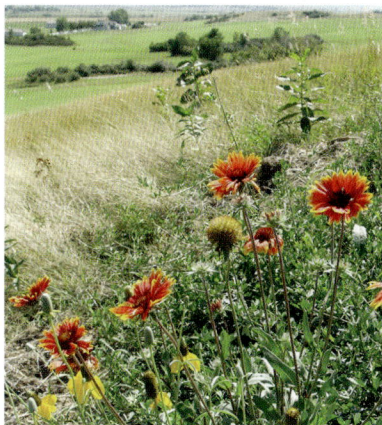
Restored Prairie

The variety of plants found in this mixed-grass prairie can be staggering. Look for depressions that hold tallgrass species like the big bluestem and Indian grass.

Moisture is more abundant here than the top of the rolling hills and you may find prickly pear cactus and yucca, plants often found in deserts.

WOODY DRAW

Cut among the rolling terrain are numerous woody draws or ravines, allowing for a different environment than you'll see on the open prairie. Here a new variety of plants grows and prospers because there is more moisture and the wildfires, for the most part, have spared them. Since such areas are dominated by trees, the wind plays only a minor here in determining the species found here.

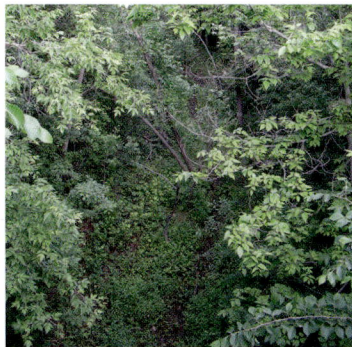
Woody draw

NATURE CHECKLISTS

Located at the confluence of the Missouri and Heart rivers, this historic park has an interesting selection of areas for wildlife watching and exploring diverse ecosystems. It is one of few Heart River floodplain areas still in a natural condition. The variety of wildlife and plants found are the result of a wide range of environments, including mixed-grass prairie, woody draws and cottonwood-dominated floodplain forests.

Birds

The rivers provide habitat for migrating waterfowl, while the uplands are home to a wide selection of song, game and predatory birds. Take a walk on the multi-use trail overlooking the floodplain or the nature trail, starting at the hillside picnic area.

Canada goose

Here are a few of the birds at Fort Abraham Lincoln State Park. See how many you can find.

☐ American redstart
☐ bald eagle
☐ black-billed magpie
☐ black-headed grosbeak
☐ broad-winged hawk
☐ brown thrasher
☐ Canada goose
☐ common tern
☐ ferruginous hawk
☐ goldfinch

☐ grasshopper sparrow
☐ least tern
☐ marsh hawk
☐ piping plover
☐ ring-billed gull
☐ ring-necked pheasant
☐ sharp-tailed grouse
☐ spotted sandpiper
☐ Sprague's pipit
☐ Swainson's hawk

Mammals

This 1,000-acre plus park is a natural refuge for a variety of mammals. There are a number of animals at Fort Abraham Lincoln State Park. Try your luck at spotting them.

Red fox

- ☐ badger
- ☐ chipmunk
- ☐ cottontail rabbit
- ☐ coyote
- ☐ gray squirrel
- ☐ ground squirrel
- ☐ porcupine

- ☐ raccoon
- ☐ red fox
- ☐ red squirrel
- ☐ skunk
- ☐ vole
- ☐ weasel
- ☐ white-tailed deer

NATURE

Plants

The diversity of plant species is a result of the varied soil and moisture conditions found throughout the park. On the mixed-grass prairie you will find plants capable of surviving harsher environments than those found on the floodplains.

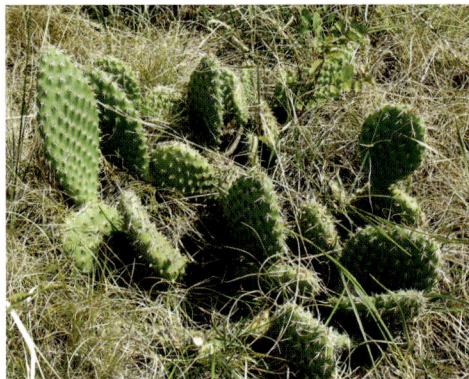
Prickly pear cactus

Check off each plant as you find it!

- ☐ American elm
- ☐ beaked hazel
- ☐ asparagus
- ☐ buffaloberry
- ☐ choke cherry
- ☐ dame's rocket
- ☐ false Solomon's seal
- ☐ gooseberry
- ☐ hemp dogbane
- ☐ Indian grass
- ☐ Juneberry
- ☐ harebell
- ☐ Kentucky bluegrass
- ☐ little bluestem
- ☐ milkwort

- ☐ needle-and-thread
- ☐ oval-leaved milkweed
- ☐ poison ivy
- ☐ porcupine grass
- ☐ red osier dogwood
- ☐ sand cherry
- ☐ stiff sunflower
- ☐ thimbleweed
- ☐ virgin's bower
- ☐ white mustard
- ☐ wild columbine
- ☐ wild grape
- ☐ wild rose
- ☐ yarrow

Blockhouse amid diverse vegetation

HISTORY

ON-A-SLANT INDIAN VILLAGE

The "Nu'Eta" or Mandan were a sedentary, agriculturally-based society and lived in earth lodge villages along the Missouri River. It was also a culture dominated by women. They built and owned the lodges and planted and tended the crops.

Scattered Corn with hoe measuring for an earth lodge

Gardens of corn, beans and squash were grown in rich soil along the river. The men went on hunting expeditions across the prairie to supply the village with meat, including bison, deer and elk. Well respected by other tribes as skillful traders, the Mandan bartered items such as grain, tobacco, pelts, tools and garden produce.

Smallpox took an extreme toll on the American Indian population and the tribes who lived in villages were especially hard hit. After the devastation of both disease and attacks from other Indian tribes, the Mandan were left with no choice but to leave their world behind.

When the Lewis and Clark expedition stopped at the ruined village site on October 20, 1804, the surviving Mandan had moved closer to the Knife River to live with the Hidatsa, a closely related tribe. Lewis and Clark camped near here as the Corps of Discovery pushed up the Missouri River.

William Duncan Strong archaeological dig at On-A-Slant Village

Reconstruction

In the 1930s the Civilian Conservation Corps (CCC) reconstructed a number of earth lodges and began working on interpretive signs for the site. After these earth lodges began to fall apart they were rebuilt in the 1970s and again in the 1990s.

Occupied 1575 to 1781

Points of Interest

- tour reconstructed ceremonial lodge and 3 earth lodges
- Mandan lifestyle and culture highlighted through interpretive programs
- self-guided interpretive tour of village site
- walk down to sunken garden north of the On-A-Slant Village; visitors will find a reconstructed Mandan garden area with a willow fence to protect it from animals; steps built by the Civilian Conservation Corps.

Interpretive Sites

Archaeological Remnants These depressions are the only visible remnants of the original Mandan earth lodges. When the Lewis and Clark expedition traveled through here in 1804 they wrote, "almost all that remains of them is the wall surrounding them and fallen areas of earth which covered the houses."

Earth Lodges Constructed out of cottonwood logs or other tree species, willow mats and a layer of grass, clay and dirt, these 20-to 40-foot structures faced the center of the village and were closely grouped together for protection. A typical earth lodge could be constructed in 10 to 17 days and lasted around 10 years.

Village Center Public gatherings, games, festivals, ceremonies, exhibits and parades were held on this circular open space. The Mandan maintained the village center's hard, pavement-like ground hard like pavement, and kept it clean and neat.

Ark Of Lone Man According to oral tradition, the Lone Man saved the Mandan Nation from a great flood covering the earth by constructing a palisade around his people. The ark or symbolic shrine is located in the village center and built out of red cedar and willow.

Ceremonial Lodge Here the Mandan performed the 4-day O-Kee-Pa, their most elaborate ceremony. The religion of the Mandan Nation looked to one supreme being, alternatively named the Lord of Life, the First Creator or the Great Spirit.

Scaffolds Three different types were used by the Mandan Nation:

- Corn Stage Scaffold–used for drying corn, meat, squash and wild fruit; constructed with 6 perpendicular poles
- Watcher's Stage Scaffold–used to guard gardens from birds and animals as crops ripened; constructed by women and children, using 4 forked posts topped with split logs and buffalo skins
- Burial Scaffold–built of 4 upright posts, 4 connecting posts and held by willow rods to hold deceased Mandan people; located in back of village

Scaffolding to dry meats and hides, also to deter dogs

FORT MCKEEN

The U.S. Army was a forceful presence on the frontier of the Dakota Territory, establishing one military fort after another as the Northern Pacific Railroad laid down its westward tracks. Fort McKeen was one of the first army posts built along the Missouri River.

Original blockhouse

As the railroad pushed across the northern Great Plains, a new fort was needed to protect the engineers and work parties. The selected site was a hilltop overlooking the Heart and Missouri rivers. Plans were to construct buildings for a two-company infantry post.

On June 14, 1872, the B and C Companies of the 6th Infantry arrived at the site to establish the new military post. Fort McKeen was named for Col. H. Boyd McKeen of the 81st Pennsylvania volunteers, killed on June 3, 1864 in the battle of Cold Harbor during the Civil War.

Reconstructed blockhouses

Under the command of Col. Daniel Huston, the men built three blockhouses and a wood stockade on two sides to protect the fort. This was the tradition of early frontier posts, which took advantage of the steep hill falling down to the floodplain of the Heart River for protection from hostile American Indian tribes. Fort McKeen's buildings were constructed from hewn logs and lumber.

Reconstructed Fort Abraham Lincoln

Infantry proved to be ineffective on the Great Plains, due to the vast amount of territory to cover. To protect railroad workers and early settlers from attacks by Indian tribes, the military decided it needed the cavalry. In addition, the fort was too far from a water source.

On November 19, 1872, the military post was renamed Fort Abraham Lincoln. By the next spring Congress authorized the construction of a cavalry post. Troops continued to be garrisoned at Fort McKeen though it became a subordinate post.

Restoration

After the fort declined in usefulness and was decommissioned, early settlers tore down the buildings and used the material in their homes and farms. In the 1930s a company of the Civilian Conservation Corps rebuilt three of the blockhouses and marked the other building locations.

Occupied 1872 to 1891
Interpretive features

- 3 blockhouses open year-round
- self-guided tour of fort foundations
- Post Cemetery located west of parking lot
- check out the view of surrounding landscape, including floodplains of the Heart and Missouri rivers and the skyline of Bismarck and Mandan including the State Capitol building

FORT ABRAHAM LINCOLN

A new fort site was authorized March 3, 1873, and construction started on a former floodplain of the Missouri River, just below the Fort McKeen infantry post. The buildings of Fort Abraham Lincoln were

Lt. Col. Custer and the 7th Cavalry

laid out around a cavalry square. This included a row of officer's quarters on the east edge of the post.

In the autumn of 1873, Lt. Col. Custer took over command of the fort along with his 7th Cavalry troops. By 1874, six companies of the 7th and three companies of the 6th and 17th infantry were stationed at Fort Abraham Lincoln. It was now one of the largest and most important forts on the northern plains, consisting of 650 infantry and cavalry soldiers.

One of the most consequential acts by Custer during his time at the post was the Black Hills Expedition of 1874. He and the 7th Cavalry traveled into the area set aside for the Dakota and discovered gold. The expedition led to the great Indian Wars of the upper Great Plains.

Reconstructed Custer House

On May 17, 1876, a force of 600 men of the 7th Cavalry under the command of Lt. Col. Custer rode west toward the valley of the Little Big Horn. Charging against a large, well-armed Indian force, many of these soldiers were killed in one of greatest defeats of the U.S. Army. By the time it was over, 263 soldiers and officers, including Custer, had perished.

As the frontier pushed farther west, Fort Abraham Lincoln began to decline in importance. Troops were transferred to newly built forts and by 1879 the headquarters for the 7th Cavalry shifted to Fort Meade. Most of the soldiers were moved down to the cavalry post and by 1881 they were beginning to dismantle the structures on the hill. It wasn't long before the fort lost any useful role in protecting the railroad workers and settlers.

Once the railroad reached the Montana line in 1883, the fort's importance rapidly declined. The last troops left Fort Abraham Lincoln and on July 23, 1891, the garrison closed. A custodian was placed in charge of the buildings after the fort transferred to the Interior Department. It didn't take long before the area settlers started to tear down the buildings. By December 1, 1894, all but three structures were dismantled.

Restoration

A Civilian Conservation Corps crew marked all the old foundations with stone in the 1930s. The effort to reconstruct a number of the fort's buildings was started in 1986 by the Fort Abraham Lincoln Foundation.

Occupied 1873 to 1891

Interpretive features

- reconstructed buildings include the Custer House, commissary, enlisted Men's Barracks, granary and stable

- guided interpretive and living history tours available in summer

- gift shop on far end of commissary building

HISTORICAL BUILDINGS

History is featured in the distinctive and various structures built by the Civilian Conservation Corps (CCC) in the 1930s and in the recently reconstructed buildings at the Cavalry Square. The CCC is well known for its log and stone structures, ranging from picnic shelters to rock walls to public buildings and you'll find a good selection here at the park. In 1986 work started on reconstructing the Custer House as a centennial project for the state of North Dakota. Today another four military buildings have been added to help interpret the history of this frontier fort.

Commanding Officer's Quarters

Commonly referred to as the Custer House, this is where Lt. Col. George Armstrong and his wife, Libbie, lived during their time at Fort Abraham Lincoln. The home was reconstructed for North Dakota's Centennial Celebration in 1989.

Custer House

There were two Custer homes during the time George and Libbie spent at the fort. The first was destroyed by fire in February of 1874. For the second house, the Custers added their own touches and considered it their only real home. On December 1, 1894, local settlers dismantled the unoccupied structure.

Today the Custer House has been reconstructed through mostly private donations and features period furnishing and artifacts. There is a large, 32-foot living room with a bay window and a sweeping veranda on two sides.

Commissary Store

Originally this building stood on the Cavalry Square from 1873 to 1885. It served as a warehouse for the fort, holding a month's rations of bacon, salt,

Commissary

beef, flour, cornmeal and hardtack. The commissary also served as a place for the soldiers to buy luxury items.

The reconstructed building is historically accurate on the outside and the interior serves a number of uses for the visitor. Inside, there is a gift shop, modern bathroom facilities, interpretive display and a large meeting room for rent.

Central Barracks

This two-building structure is a reconstructed facility which recreates what life was like for the average soldier of the 1870s trying to survive the harsh conditions of the Dakota Territory.

Interior barracks

The third building rebuilt on the Cavalry Square, it is partially furnished with objects an enlisted soldier had at his disposal. The barracks were a combined mess hall and living quarters for both non-commissioned officers and troopers of the 7th Cavalry.

Granary

This was one of the more important buildings at a cavalry post because it stored the grain for the horses. Built of rough-hewn timbers, it stored enough grain for 600 horses and mules.

During summer months, visitors can enjoy an evening performance of the Melodrama produced by the Fort Abraham

Granary

Lincoln Dramatic Association. The building also holds modern bathroom facilities and an exhibit area.

Stable

The most recent building added to the cavalry post, this represents one of six stables found at the original Fort Abraham Lincoln. Today visitors can learn how the horse and mule played an important role in the cavalry.

Interior of stables

CCC Buildings

The Civilian Conservation Corps (CCC) started work on a number of projects at the park in 1934, including reconstruction of earth lodges and building a stone museum structure. These young men rebuilt the old military road, a number of picnic shelters and marked the location of the various fort buildings.

Museum/Caretaker's Quarters

This was one of the last buildings to be constructed by the CCC, and utilizes native granite cut from large glacial boulders found within the park. Inside the building you will find native stone on the floors and locally cut cottonwood logs throughout.

Park office building

The original exhibits and displays were designed by the National Park Service and built as a Works Progress Administration (WPA) project. The value of the building was appraised at $75,000 after construction was finished. In addition, they constructed a maintenance shop and gift store.

Picnic Shelters

The Civilian Conservation Corps (CCC) built three picnic areas in the 1930s. The major area was built on the floodplain of the Heart River. In the uplands, two separate picnic areas were constructed near Fort McKeen and the On-A-Slant Village site.

Triple Shelter located on the Heart River floodplain, its unique design allows it to be used by up to three different groups of people at one time. It is built of native rock and cottonwood. A small brick shelter and round shelter are nearby.

Hillside shelter

Hillside Picnic Shelter built into the steep hillsides of the Fort McKeen site, this wooden structure sits above the former main park road. Stone steps lead visitors up to the shelter.

Fort McKeen Shelter constructed of native stone, this shelter is also located below Fort McKeen in a former woody draw.

Fort McKeen Blockhouses

After locating parts of the original foundations, three blockhouses were built from rough-hewn logs. To retain accuracy, the design was laid out using photographs and military drawings. Today the blockhouses are the result of a second recon-

McKeen picnic shelter and blockhouse

struction effort in the 1970s, after the Civilian Conservation Corps (CCC) structures began to fall apart and were declared safety hazards.

Earth Lodges

The Civilian Conservation Corps (CCC) rebuilt five earth lodges, all facing the central enclosure. There was one small dwelling, three medium-sized structures, and a large ceremonial lodge. Over the years the five original lodges fell into disrepair and were reconstructed twice, in the 1970s and 1990s.

PARK HISTORY

After the abandonment of Fort Abraham Lincoln by the military, the post was neglected for close to 30 years. President Theodore Roosevelt deeded 75 acres to the state of North Dakota in 1907 for a public park, but development didn't begin until a Civilian Conservation Corps (CCC) camp was assigned to Fort Abraham Lincoln in the 1930s. This crew of young men built a number of facilities including a museum, picnic shelters and reconstructed blockhouses and earth lodges. In the last 20 years the park has seen another phase of major development with the assistance of the Fort Abraham Lincoln Foundation. The non-profit organization has brought in both private money and federal funds to build a number of structures based on the history of Cavalry Square and the Indian Village sites.

The Beginnings

On March 2, 1907 an act of Congress transferred most of the area once occupied by the fort to North Dakota. A total of 75.5 acres was given to the State Historical Society of North Dakota to be managed as a historical park and the deed was signed by the President in 1909. This new park included portions of Fort McKeen, Fort Abraham Lincoln and the On-A-Slant Village site.

For the first 25-plus years, there were no funds for improving the site and little use by the public. In the 1930s, the country suffered through a devastating depression and drought, but one bright spot was the creation of the Civilian Conservation Corps (CCC) and other federal work programs, which sought to to improve historical and recreational sites throughout the United States.

Civilian Conservation Corps constructing an earth lodge

The Civilian Conservation Corps implemented major changes at Fort Abraham Lincoln State Park from 1934 to October 1941. Projects included reconstructing five earth lodges and a moat at the On-A-Slant Village. Archeological investigations were conducted in other portions of the site. Most of the work was under the direction of Mrs. Scattercorn, an elderly Mandan woman.

On the Fort McKeen site, workers rebuilt three wooden blockhouses, and surveyed and marked the other building locations. The men also surveyed and marked many of the former building sites at the cavalry post and repaired the old military road, gateways and parade ground.

CCC project

A number of new structures were added to the state park for visitors' enjoyment. One of the finest facilities built was a native stone Museum and Caretaker's building across the way from the On-A-Slant Village. Further construction included a concession building, picnic shelters, roads, shop, stone walls and a complex bridge.

An additional 240.2 acres was purchased during this time. In 1938, 50,000 people visited the state park. By 1942 the last of the Civilian Conservation Corps projects were discontinued, and WW II effectively ended any major development at Fort Abraham Lincoln State Park.

Continued Development

From the 1950s through the 1970s a number of major projects were completed, including designating camping sites along the floodplain of the Heart and Missouri rivers.

Historical tour in the 1970s

In the 1960s the ceremonial lodge was renovated. The military road was paved and a fence built around the cemetery site. In addition, a campground with 95 sites was finished.

The headquarters of the North Dakota Park Service was moved out to the park in 1970. A number of interpretive programs were initiated during this decade, including a living history drama, summer amphitheater program and a self-guided nature trail.

Hillside slide on north entrance road

A new wave of development started with the reconstruction of the Custer House in 1987. Further projects included building replicas of the commissary, enlisted men's barracks and granary during the 1990s. Funds from the federal government also helped rebuild a number of earth lodges at the On-A-Slant Village, including a ceremonial lodge.

Fort Abraham Lincoln also experienced a major change due to the weather. When the north entrance road began to crack and slide downward with the hillside, it was closed for safety reasons. The public now enters the park from the south only. In 2004 a reconstructed horse stable opened to the public.

Centennial Historical Timeline

1575–1781 Mandan Indians—skilled farmers and traders—live in the On-A-Slant Village along the Heart River. A combination of devastating smallpox epidemics and attacks by other tribes forced the village members to abandon their home and move north.

October 20, 1804 *"After making 12 miles, we camped on the south at the upper part of a bluff containing stone coal of an inferior quality. Immediately below this bluff are the remains of a village covering six or eight acres, formerly occupied by the Mandan, who, says our Ricara chief, lived in a number of villages on both sides of the river, until the Sioux forced them 40 miles higher; whence after a few years, they moved to their present location."* Lewis and Clark discover On-A-Slant Village, former home of the Mandan.

June 14, 1872 Companies of the U.S. Army 6th Infantry begin construction of Fort McKeen on the bluffs overlooking the Missouri and Heart rivers. They are charged with protection of Northern Pacific Railroad workers.

March 3, 1873 Cavalry troops are deemed essential by the U.S. military in the battle with hostile Indian tribes. This results in the building of a new post below Fort McKeen for the 7th Cavalry. The resulting complex is named Fort Abraham Lincoln. In the fall of 1873, famed Civil War hero Lt. Col. George Armstrong Custer arrives as the fort's new commander.

May 17, 1876 The 7th Cavalry under the command of Lt. Col. George Custer rides out of Fort Abraham Lincoln toward the Little Bighorn River. More than 260 of the men, including Custer, will never return.

May 28, 1891 With most of the Indian tribes forced onto reservations there was no need for Fort Abraham Lincoln, and it was closed by order of the U.S. Army. Homesteaders and others take it upon themselves to dismantle many of the fort buildings. They use the borrowed materials for their own homes and farms.

March 2, 1907 Under order of President Theodore Roosevelt, the fort and 75 acres are deeded to the State of North Dakota. It is placed under the State Historical Society of North Dakota, but there is little development until the 1930s.

1934 During the Great Depression, the National Park Service works with the State Legislature of North Dakota to develop a state park system. The State Legislature purchases 240 acres of land to help with the development of Fort Abraham Lincoln State Park, including the areas holding the infantry and cavalry posts.

Many of the unique structures found at Fort Abraham Lincoln are built by the Civilian Conservation Corps.

1965 The newly formed North Dakota Park Service takes over the management of Fort Abraham Lincoln State Park.

1988 The Fort Abraham Lincoln Foundation, in conjunction with the North

Constructing the Custer House

Dakota Parks and Recreation Department, starts an ambitious plan to reconstruct a number of key historical buildings at the cavalry post. Over the next two decades a variety of structures are built including the Custer House, commissary, granary, enlisted men's barracks and stable. Other work has included a ceremonial lodge at the On-A-Slant Village.

FORT LINCOLN

The two "Fort Lincolns" have confused many people, including historians. After the U.S. Army closed the original Fort Abraham Lincoln, state leaders began to advocate for the construction of a new military fort in North Dakota. Located in southern Bismarck, the new Fort Lincoln was authorized in 1896 to replace the abandoned cavalry post—Fort Abraham Lincoln.

It was occupied in 1903 as a permanent post for four infantry companies and four cavalry companies. In the beginning, people thought this new fort would be as important as Fort Snelling in Minnesota. Unfortunately, (without the political clout) there was no longer a need for a full-time military presence in the state.

During the early 1900s it served as a garrison for a small number of troops but didn't see a lot of activity until the World Wars of the twentieth century. It served as a mobilization center for North Dakota National Guard troops during the First World War. In World War II it became an internment camp for German and Japanese nationals.

As the military began to abandon Fort Lincoln for good, a number of the buildings were used by various federal and state agencies. In the early stages of the Garrison Dam construction, it was the Corps of Engineers' headquarters. Later the North Dakota Game and Fish Department and Highway Department leased a number of the buildings. Today it is used as a United Tribes employment training center.

Historic buildings at Fort Lincoln in Bismarck

NEARBY/WHILE IN THE AREA

DOUBLE DITCH STATE RECREATION AREA

Located on a floodplain between the Missouri River and the state historical site (below), the recreation area offers visitors the chance to learn about the area's history, take a walk along the river and enjoy a picnic with the Square Buttes in the background.

Location from Bismarck take River Road north for 4 miles and continue in the same direction on ND Hwy. 1804. You can access the site on the north end of Double Ditch.

Paved trail for recreation

Features paved, multi-use (non-motorized) trail running along a free-flowing Missouri River with 3 interpretive panels and picnic areas

Open year-round

Size 116 acres

Contact ND Parks and Recreation, 701-328-5357

DOUBLE DITCH INDIAN VILLAGE STATE HISTORIC SITE

Located on a scenic bluff overlooking the Missouri River, this Mandan village site is named for two dry moats surrounding 158 earth lodge depressions.

Location from Bismarck take River Road north for 4 miles, continue in same direction on ND Hwy. 1804, the site is on west side of road.

Features remains of earth lodge floors, storage pits and parts of outer fortification ditch. A small fieldstone shelter and interpretive signs are located on southwest edge. Take a walk on the interpretive trail.

Open year-round

Contact State Historical Society of ND, 701-328-2666

Civilian Conservation Corps interpretive shelter

FORMER GOVERNORS' MANSION STATE HISTORIC SITE

This stick-style Victorian mansion served 21 chief executives and their families from 1893 to 1960. Built in 1884 as a private residence, the home was purchased for $5,000 by the state and became one of the first houses in Bismarck to have indoor plumbing. In 1960, a new ranch-style residence was

Former governors' mansion

constructed on the Capitol Grounds and continues to serve as home to North Dakota governors.

Location from Fort Lincoln take 1806 north to Mandan, take I-94 east into Bismarck, then Tyler Parkway Exit south after crossing the Missouri River, at 4th Street turn south to corner of Avenue B
Features Tours and video programs of the mansion's history and restoration are available. Admission is free though donations are welcomed. Volunteers of the State Historical Society staff the mansion.
Hours daily May 16–Sept 15
Contact State Historical Society of ND, 701-328-2666

CAMP HANCOCK STATE HISTORICAL SITE

Originally developed as a U.S. infantry post in 1872, this site also served a number of different functions. From 1877 to 1894 it was a quartermaster depot and signal office. The U.S. Weather Bureau took over the site after the post was decommissioned in 1894. For most of the 1940s the U.S. Soil Conservation Service was based here. Today it is a state historical site.

Executive quarters

Location from Former Governors' Mansion follow 4th street south to Main Ave., turn west (right), located at 101 East Main Avenue
Features post executive quarters, St. George's Episcopal Church and a vintage 1909 railroad locomotive
Open May 16–Sept 15
Contact State Historical Society of North Dakota, 701-328-2666

STEAMBOAT WAREHOUSE STATE HISTORIC SITE

This interpretive site marks the location of a warehouse built by the Northern Pacific Railway. The stone and frame warehouse stored goods being shipped by steamboat and train.

From this site take a hike along the Missouri River to the keelboat and steamboat parks. Children of all ages will enjoy climbing on a scale replica of the keelboat used by Lewis and Clark on their 1804-'06 expedition, or explore the steamboat replica.

Location from Camp Hancock follow Main Avenue west to River Road, turn north (right) and follow it to the site located along the Missouri River
Features a fieldstone monument and interpretive information
Contact State Historical Society of North Dakota, 701-328-2666

Stone marker

NORTH DAKOTA VETERANS' CEMETERY

Established in 1989 by an act of the Legislative Assembly, the cemetery is "dedicated to the men and women who have served this state and nation with unequaled distinction and honor."

Overall view

On July 6, 1992, the initial interment took place at the first national cemetery in North Dakota. A major portion of the construction work was done by National Guard engineering units and accomplished with private funds.

> **Location** southwest corner of Fort Abraham Lincoln State Park, entrance gate found off ND Hwy. 1806
> **Size** 35 acres
> **Contact** North Dakota National Guard, P.O. Box 5511, Bismarck, ND 58506; 701-667-1418

FORT RICE STATE HISTORIC SITE

This is one of the first army forts built west of the Missouri River to establish a military presence on the frontier. General Alfred H. Sully selected the location for the fort during an 1864 expedition. Fort Rice turned into one of the most highly

Foundations of former buildings

active forts in the Dakota Territory. On November 25, 1878, the fort was abandoned after Fort Yates was built.

Location from state park take ND Hwy. 1806 south for 17 miles
Features Includes visible remnants from the old fort, including depressions, foundation lines and Works Progress Administration (WPA) corner markers. There is also an interpretive marker with a map and parking space. Trail head location for a 17-mile snowmobile trail to Fort Abraham Lincoln.
Open daily May 16–Sept 15
Contact State Historical Society of North Dakota, 701-328-2666

HUFF INDIAN VILLAGE STATE HISTORIC SITE

Once home to the Mandan, this prehistoric village was home to nearly 1,000 people around 1500 AD. The Huff Village is one of the most pristine Indian sites in North Dakota. Visitors will still be able to see remnants of the earth lodges and defensive structures. Listed on the National Register of Historic Sites, it has never been plowed.

Visitors looking at interpretive sign

Location from Fort Abraham Lincoln State Park take ND Hwy. 1806 south 12 miles, site on east side of highway next to the town of Huff
Features remains of collapsed rectangular dwellings and a fortification ditch, interpretive marker with a map
Open daily May 16–Sept 15
Contact State Historical Society of North Dakota, 701-328-2666

WARD VILLAGE OVERLOOK

This village was home to the Mandan from around 1500 AD until it was abandoned prior to the year 1800. During the time of the Mandan, this village was protected by a deep ditch and log palisade.

Enjoying the overlook

Located on a prominent hilltop, the site offers a sweeping view of the river and the city of Mandan.

Location in Pioneer Park on Burnt Boat Drive, off Exit 157 on I-94 in northwest Bismarck
Features earth lodge depressions and ditch, self-guided interpretive walking trail
Open year-round
Contact State Historical Society of North Dakota, 701-328-2666

MENOKEN INDIAN VILLAGE STATE HISTORIC SITE

One of the first semi-perma-nent villages in the state, the Menoken site was occupied for 200 years from 1000–1200 AD. Lodges at this site were oval instead of the usual round shape found at Mandan villages. According to the State

CCC Interpretive Site

Historical Society of North Dakota, there are about 20 lodges on 2.5 acres. A national historic landmark, the site is located along the Apple River.

Location 10 miles east of Bismarck on north side of I-94, near the town of Menoken
Features lodge depressions and a bastioned fortification ditch, along with a fieldstone kiosk containing maps and brief interpretive information.
Open year-round
Contact State Historical Society of ND, 701-328-2666

NORTH DAKOTA HERITAGE CENTER

The natural and human narrative of North Dakota is told here through an amazing collection of displays, artifacts and stories. Inside the permanent gallery you can check out the tusks of a giant mastodon, the artistic flair of American

Heritage Center

Indian clothing and the Dakota Kids area, where children can touch the hides of wildlife or ride toy horses. The Heritage Center is also the ideal stop for doing research on your family or North Dakota.

Location From Fort Lincoln take 1806 north to Mandan and get on I-94 heading east to Bismarck. Take Exit 159 off I-94 onto State Street, State Capitol grounds located on west side just after Divide Avenue.

Features Houses rotating exhibits, special events, gift shop and the State Archives and Historical Research Library. The Heritage Center also holds the facilities for the divisions of archeology, historic preservation, education and interpretation and historic sites. Look for the Sakakawea statue near the entrance, the water fountain in the front plaza and the large cottonwood tree.

Hours weekdays 8–5, Sat 9–5 and Sun 11–5

Contact State Historical Society of ND, 701-328-2666, www.ndtourism.com

STATE CAPITOL AND GROUNDS

Driving into the capital city of Bismarck, it's hard to miss this 19-story, Art Deco building—called the "skyscraper on the prairie." Built of white Indiana limestone, the capitol building was constructed for $2 million in the early 1930s after fire destroyed the original capitol structure on the night of December 28, 1930.

Inside, visitors will marvel at an interior featuring Belgium black marble, Honduras mahogany, Indian rosewood and Burma teak. The building is 241.5 feet tall. In addition to the State Heritage Center

Interior of the State Capitol

you will find numerous historical structures, the Liberty Memorial Building with the state library and the North Dakota governors' residence.

Location 600 East Boulevard Avenue

Features "Theodore Roosevelt Rough Rider Hall of Fame" in the ground floor lobby of the capitol building. A series of oil portraits highlight notable North Dakotans for accomplishments that have brought honor to the state.

Tours of the State Capitol weekdays on the hour from 8–11 am and 1–4 pm year-round. From Memorial Day to Labor Day, tours are available on Saturdays from 9–4 and Sundays from 1–4. Tours include a trip up to the 18th-floor observation deck. There is no charge for the tour.

Capitol Grounds

This 132-acre, park-like area surrounds the capitol building and features statues, memorials, trails and parks. Visitors may hike the two trails—Arboretum Trail and Prairie Trail, enjoy the playground and basketball court in Capitol Park, and walk through the Centennial Tree Grove.

Take A Look

All Veterans Centennial Memorial located south of the Heritage Center, this memorial is dedicated to all North Dakotans who served in the armed forces during the first 100 years of statehood.

French Gratitude Boxcar Donated by people of France on February 9, 1949, the boxcar transported soldiers during World War I and World War II in France.

John Burke Statue Located in front of the Capitol Building. John Burke served as a state legislator and governor from 1907-1913, as Supreme Court Justice from 1925-1937 and as U.S. Treasurer. A second statue of John Burke sits in the rotunda of the U.S. Capitol Building.

Arboretum Trail This nature trail highlights environmental, artistic and architectural features on the capitol grounds. Check out the approximately 75 different species of trees and shrubs highlighted with markers. The trail also includes petrified sequoia stumps.

John Burke Statue

Arboretum Trail

Prairie Trail Located southwest of the Capitol Building, this trail features native prairie grasses and wildflowers.

Sakakawea Statue Located north of the Heritage Center, this statue honors Sakakawea, the Shoshone Indian woman who helped guide the Lewis and Clark expedition from Fort Mandan to the Yellowstone River in 1805.

ND Capitol and Grounds Historical Timeline

June 2, 1883 City of Bismarck becomes the capital of Dakota Territory.

1883 A red brick structure is constructed on a high bluff overlooking the Missouri River to serve at the first capitol building.

November 2, 1889 Legislation signed by President Benjamin Harrison brings North Dakota into the union, along with South Dakota.

1920-24 Over this four-year period, the Liberty Memorial Building is constructed using a federal-style design. In 1982, the state library moves into the building after it is remodeled.

December 28, 1930 Fire destroys the first capitol building after the spontaneous combustion of oily rags in a janitor's closet.

August 13, 1932 A ground-breaking ceremony takes place for a new capitol building, officiated by Governor George F. Shafer.

September 5, 1933 On the 50th anniversary of the dedication of the first capitol building, a cornerstone for the new building is laid.

1934 Construction is completed on the new building, which features white Indiana limestone.

January, 1935 The new capitol building is first occupied.

1960 A new governors' residence is completed on the state capitol grounds. Governor John E. Davis is the first to live in this 18-room, ranch-style house, which is built out of bricks from North Dakota.

1973 The state capitol undergoes major remodeling.

1981 A new judicial wing is built to provide offices for the State Supreme Court, along with other agencies.

1981 The North Dakota Heritage Center opens on the state Capitol grounds.

Contact 701-328-2480; www.discovernd.com

BISMARCK CITY TRAIL SYSTEM

The capital city features more than 30 miles of recreational trails open to the public for walking, jogging, biking, in-line skating and other non-motorized activities. This trail system will connect you to the Double Ditch State Recreation Area and Historic Site. For a map of the trails, visit www.bisparks.org/ParksAndTrails/trails.asp.

Trails

4.13-mile Hay Creek Trail
3.60-mile Riverwood Golf Course Loop
3.20-mile Sertoma Park Loop
3.04-mile Pioneer Park to expressway
2.50-mile Solheim School to Wachter Middle School
2.40-mile Tom O'Leary Golf Course
2.16-mile 26th Street/Divide Avenue/Sleepy Hollow Park/Rosser Avenue
1.61-mile Pebble Creek Loop
1.00-mile Cottonwood Park Loop
0.75-mile Chief Looking's Village
0.38-mile Igoe Park Loop

Chief Looking's Earth Lodge Village Interpretive Trail

This former Mandan earth lodge village features a 3/4-mile self-guided interpretive trail highlighting earth lodge depressions and a fortification ditch. The Mandan lived in this village dating back to 1675.

Location Pioneer Park Overlook off Burnt Boat Drive

Contact State Historical Society of North Dakota, 701-328-2666

MANDAN CITY TRAIL SYSTEM

Connected with the trail system of her sister city, Mandan has an additional 11 miles of trails and takes you to Fort Abraham Lincoln State Park on the Millennium Legacy Trail. This recently paved trail system allows users to walk, in-line skate, skateboard, bike and jog.

The 1.6-mile trail starts at the corner of Third Street and Sixth Avenue SE, near the Stage Stop. It takes you to the soccer fields of Dacotah Centennial Park and near the Prairie West Golf Course.

The 1.8-mile trail begins at the Dacotah Centennial Park and continues all the way to 46th Avenue SE. Enjoy the benches and trees, added to improve the trail's features.

Mandan trail system

The 3-mile scenic trail along the Heart River begins south of the Stage Stop and connects with trails at Fort Abraham Lincoln State Park on the north boundary.

A hiking and mountain biking trail is located at Sunset Park, north of the Mandan Community Center. This rough-terrain trail loops through the 80-acre park.

The Missouri River Nature Area also features a hiking/mountain biking trail. Located east and south of the archery range, this trail follows the flat terrain of the river bottoms. Check out the diverse selection of wildlife at both areas.

DAKOTA ZOO

This modern facility features more than 500 mammals, birds and reptiles, representing over 125 different species. Visitors will find many native animals including bison, prairie dogs and mountain lions. The Dakota Zoo also showcases numerous exotic animals such as small cotton-top tamarins and the two-humped bactrian camels. The zoo has been an accredited member of the American Zoo and Aquarium Association (AZA) since 1991.

Location Sertoma Park on the Missouri River in Bismarck on Riverside Park Road

Animals include moose, mountain goat, black bear, bobcat, river otter and lynx

Features Tribune Discovery Center with animal presentations, speakers, day camps for kids, zoo overnight camps, summer flashlight tours, storytime with the animals, special events, antler trading post, children's play area, the Tribune and Leach Express, along with a concession stand

Hours daily 10 am–8 pm from late April–Sept 30; throughout the rest of the year Fri–Sun, 1–5

Contact 701-223-7543; www.dakotazoo.org

LEWIS & CLARK RIVERBOAT

Ride in comfort and style on this replica paddle wheeler down the Missouri River. Choose from afternoon and evening trips that feature historical narration of the river

Lewis & Clark Riverboat

and Bismarck-Mandan region. This is the last 150-passenger vessel on the Upper Missouri River.

Location Port of Bismarck at 1700 North River Road, off Exit 157 on I-94

Features group rates, climate controlled lower deck, licensed bar, snacks, 2 restrooms, a smoke-free environment, a gift shop, bicycle rentals and charitable gambling.

Hours Memorial Day to Labor Day weekends. Charter cruises available April through October

Contact 701-255-4233

FIVE NATIONS ARTS

A large selection of American Indian arts and crafts are available at Five Nations Arts in the historic Burlington Northern Railroad Depot. Inside you will find works from more than 200 American Indian artists from North Dakota. Artists are encouraged to use traditional techniques and natural materials. Look for jewelry, dream catchers, original oil paintings, sculptures, baskets, buffalo robes and raw materials.

Location 401 West Main Street in Mandan

Features extended hours in summer and during the Christmas season

Hours open May–Oct, Mon–Sat, 9–7, Sun, 12–5; Nov–April, Mon–Sat, 9–5:30, Sun, 12–5

Five Nations Art Center

Contact 701-663-4663, www.5nationsart.com

NORTH DAKOTA STATE RAILROAD MUSEUM

Home of North Dakota's railroad history, the museum features exhibits and artifacts from the early 1900s. Visitors will find intricate models, photographs and uniforms on display. Originally the museum building was used as the yard office for the Burlington Northern Railroad in Mandan.

Location north of Mandan on Old Red Trail at 3102 37th Street Northwest

Features Maintains 11 displays of train cars along with 5 acres of railroad artifacts and equipment. Gift Shop sells an assortment of railroad memorabilia including shirts, caps, postcards, books, and more. The museum features an extensive collection of photographs from Ron V. Nixon, a longtime Northern Pacific dispatcher.

Hours daily 1–5 Memorial Day through Labor Day

Contact 701-663-9322; www.geocities.com/ndsrm

BUCKSTOP JUNCTION

This reconstructed village features a number of historical buildings from the late 1800s through the early 1930s. Visitors will enjoy the atmosphere of a community from the turn of the twentieth century on this 20-acre site. Bring your family or school group to learn firsthand about the life of a North Dakotan before the time of telephones, TVs or other modern conveniences—including running water!

Location Missouri Valley Fairgrounds east of Bismarck Expressway

Features a mining camp complete with coal mine, gas shovel, scale house and mine building; site established and designed by the Missouri Valley Historical Society

Contact 701-255-4205 or 701-223-4838

Buckstop Junction

NORTH DAKOTA GAME AND FISH LOBBY WILDLIFE MUSEUM

North Dakota fish and wildlife are on display at the headquarters lobby of the Game and Fish Department. Visitors should also check out the Outdoor Wildlife Learning Site, featuring a fishing pond and interpretive walking trail.

Location Game and Fish Department headquarters, 100 N. Bismarck Expressway, Bismarck, ND

Features the Outdoor Wildlife Learning Site (OWLS) highlights efforts to improve wildlife habitat in an outdoor learning center atmosphere. The 55-acre site includes fishing access, interpretive trails and the demonstration of wildlife habitat enhancement techniques.

Hours Mon–Fri, 8–5

Contact 701-328-6300; gf.nd.gov/

Outdoor Learning Site at the North Dakota Game and Fish Museum

GATEWAY TO SCIENCE

Experience the magic of science through hands-on exhibits designed for children of all ages. Learn how the world works through the understanding of science. This is a great way to be exposed to new principles not found in most classroom settings.

Location 1810 Schafer Street, Suite 1 at the Frances Leach High Prairie Arts and Science Complex, north of Bismarck State College campus

Features Offers high-quality activities and exhibits for teachers, students and the general public. This includes interactive exhibits, special programs for students and special events for the general public.

Air Pressure–Explore the collection of exhibits demonstrating different concepts regarding air pressure, including the Bottle Rocket, Bernoulli Effect and Air Cannon displays

Light & Color–Twenty-four hands-on exhibits demonstrate the principles and effects of light, color, vision and lasers

Electricity & Magnetism–Learn about electrical currents, circuits, electrical fields and magnetism.

Open Mon–Thurs, 12–7, Fri–Sat, 12–5

Contact 701-258-1975; gscience@gscience.org; www.gscience.org

RESOURCES

SUPPORT GROUPS

Fort Abraham Lincoln Foundation

Custer House Dedication

An important partner in the ongoing development and interpretation of Fort Abraham Lincoln State Park, the foundation was originally formed in the 1980s to rebuild the Custer Home. Today the Fort Abraham Lincoln Foundation works with the park staff and other agencies to recreate a historical view of the Cavalry Square and On-A-Slant Mandan Indian Village. The foundation and park jointly manage an interpretive program for the two historic sites, providing tours of the Custer House, assorted fort buildings and the earth lodge complex. To help celebrate the diversity of culture found at Fort Abraham Lincoln, a number of special events and programs are offered for visitors of all ages. The Fort Abraham Lincoln Foundation prides itself on operating the "finest living history program on the Northern Plains."

It works hand in hand with park staff to develop, coordinate and present interpretive programs about the Mandan tribe and 7th Cavalry. As a member-supported foundation, it is dedicated to preserving and promoting the heritage of the historic properties of Fort Abraham Lincoln State Park and other historical sites of North Dakota.

Single and family memberships are available, offering a variety of benefits including discounts and annual passes.

Established in 1982 to reconstruct the Custer House for the 1989 North Dakota Centennial

Contact Historic Mandan Depot, 401 West Main, Mandan, ND 58554; 701-663-4758; info@fortlincoln.com

Family or Single Membership per year fee

Members receive an annual pass to Fort Abraham Lincoln State Park, free tickets to Fort Abraham Lincoln's summer theatre, *The Past Times* (newsletters), and a 10% discount at the Commissary Bookstore and Five Nations Arts

NORTH DAKOTA PARKS AND RECREATION DEPT.

This mostly rural state is blessed with a system of 17 state parks and recreation areas. Visitors will find amazing scenery, varied outdoor recreational amenities, important wildlife habitat, protection of cultural and natural resources, and the tranquility that helps relieve the stress of everyday life.

Contact

NDPR Department Headquarters
1600 Century Avenue
Bismarck, ND 58503
701-328-5357, parkrec@nd.gov
www.parkrec.nd.gov

Historical Tour of Fort Abraham Lincoln

INDEX

NOTES

NOTES

ABOUT THE AUTHOR

Everyone should learn something from their 2, year-old niece. Jenny reminded Scott why it is good to go with the flow of the wind (she loved to run with the wind but hated going against it). This is how he became a park ranger and stuck with it for almost 15 years. Scott discovered the wonderful world of wetlands at Lake Metigoshe and fell into a new career of advocating a need to restore, improve and protect our natural environment. Today, Scott is lucky to have a job where one day he is sampling macroinvertebrates to determine water quality and the next teaching children the importance of watershed boundaries and on another day he's off exploring by paddling rivers with a diverse selection of experts. As a result of the winds blowing him east, Scott and his partner and best friend, Angie, now live in southern Minnesota and enjoy going on new adventures wherever the breeze might push them.

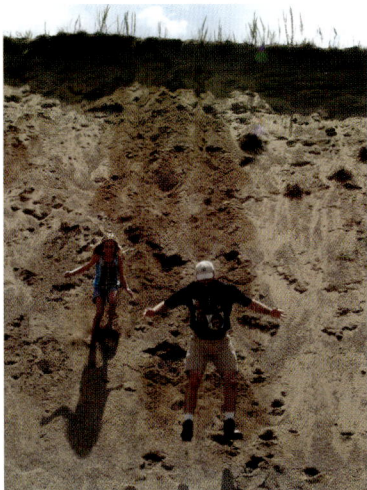

Scott and Jenny at Cross Ranch State Park